'Do This In Memory of Me'

Most of the material in this book originally appeared in
Spirituality as a series of articles entitled,
Jesus' Table Companionship.
Spirituality is published six times a year by Dominican
Publications, Dublin.

'DO THIS IN MEMORY OF ME'

Reflections on the Eucharist in the light of Jesus' Table-Companionship

Pierre Simson M. Afr.

Dominican Publications
Dublin

First published (2003) by
Dominican Publications
42 Parnell Square
Dublin 1

ISBN 1-871552-82-6

Cover design by Bill Bolger

Printed in Ireland by
The Leinster Leader, Naas, Co. Kildare.

Cover. Detail from a stone carving of Wicklow granite commissioned by
Sr Caoimhín O.P., founder of the Matt Talbot Community Trust, to
represent the spirit and activities of the trust's work in Ballinascorney, Co.
Dublin. The Trust operates a centre where men come on day release from
prison.

Featured are loaves and fishes, (the logo of the Trust),
a communal meal, a bus, work in the garden, football.
(See back cover)

CONTENTS

Introduction

Circumstances, in the past twenty years, have led me to focus my attention more and more on the Gospels; on 'Jesus, the only begotten Son who is nearest to the Father's heart' (John 1:18) and whose mission it is to tell us who the Father is. And among the many treasures I have found in my study and teaching of the Gospels, one of the richest has been Jesus' table-companionship, which I now see as a necessary angle from which to approach the Eucharist, 'the memorial of Jesus' death and resurrection' (*Sacrosanctum Concilium* 47).

I have already had the joy of sharing this treasure with many people, in Africa, in Jerusalem, and lately in Ireland; I would like now to invite the readers of these pages to come and sit with me at 'the table of the Word' to look at Jesus, to listen to him, and to let him open to us more fully the mystery of the Eucharist.

But first I would like to reflect a little on the place of the Eucharist in the Church, and in our own lives.

CHAPTER ONE

From the Eucharist to Jesus' Meals

Vatican II and the Eucharist

Assessing the place and meaning of the Eucharist in the life of the Church, the council of Vatican II had wonderful things to say: 'At the Last Supper, on the night he was betrayed , our Saviour instituted the Eucharistic sacrifice of his Body and Blood. This he did in order to perpetuate the sacrifice of the Cross throughout the ages until he should come again, and so to entrust to his Beloved Spouse, the Church, a memorial of his death and resurrection: a sacrament of love, a sign of unity, a bond of charity, a paschal banquet in which Christ is consumed, the mind is filled with grace, and a pledge of future glory is given to us' (Constitution on the Liturgy, *Sacrosanctum Concilium* 47).

To vowed religious, the Council had this to say: 'Your communities, since they are united in Christ's name, naturally have as their centre the Eucharist, the Sacrament of Love, the sign of unity and the bond of charity' (Apostolic Exhortation on the Renewal of Religious Life, *Evangelica Testificatio*, n. 48).

And finally, to priests: 'No Christian community is built up which does not grow from and hinge on the celebration of the most holy Eucharist. From this, all education for community spirit must begin' (Decree on the Life and Ministry of Priests, *Presbyterorum Ordinis*, n. 6).

These texts obviously echo what always been in some way the teaching of the Church, but they highlight a dimension which was not always given sufficient attention: the community dimension. The

Eucharist is, of course, 'a paschal banquet in which Christ is consumed, the mind is filled with grace, and a pledge of future glory is given to us'; it is also, always, 'a sacrament of love, a sign of unity, a bond of charity...; it is the centre of the Christian community...; from the Eucharist, all education for community spirit must begin.' We cannot truly participate in the Eucharist, unless we approach it in a spirit of communion with our community, with people.

Against the background of the situation of Christian communities today, throughout the world, this teaching of Vatican II cannot but raise important and even disturbing questions: if it is true that 'no Christian community is built up which does not grow from and hinge on the celebration of the most Holy Eucharist', what are we to think of the innumerable Christian communities which are deprived of the Eucharist because there are no priests available to celebrate it? What are we to think of the many Christians who would willingly participate fully in the Eucharist, but cannot, because of the situation in which they live? We may not be in a position to solve such grave problems; but we are certainly urgently asked to be aware of them, and never to feel satisfied with our eucharistic practice until, in accordance with Jesus' desire, we are truly one – one family, not just invited to the Lord's table, but able to share the Body and Blood of the Lord.

Our Personal Experience of the Eucharist

Whatever the teaching of the Church may be, what is my personal experience of the Eucharist? Why do I participate in the Eucharist? What do I seek in the celebration of the Eucharist? Do I feel that my experience is in harmony with the teaching of Vatican II on the Eucharist or, on the contrary, am I under the impression that the Council texts do not really mean much to me? And why is that? Am I now willing to spend some time to let Jesus' words in the gospels challenge me, and open wider for me the riches of the Eucharist?

From Eucharist to the Last Supper, and to Jesus' Meals

In the Church's tradition, especially since the Council of Trent (1545-1563), the Eucharist has been presented mainly, if not exclusively, as *sacrifice*. And any biblical investigation into the origin and meaning of our present day Eucharists was focused on the Last Supper, the last

meal shared by Jesus with his disciples: 'At the Last Supper, on the
night that he was betrayed, our Saviour instituted the eucharistic
sacrifice of his Body and Blood' (Constitution on the Liturgy,
Sacrosanctum Concilium, n. 47).

But we must not forget that the 'Last Supper' was precisely the last of
a whole history of 'suppers' that Jesus shared with 'his own' and with
others (Elisabeth A. Johnson, *Consider Jesus,* Crossroads, 1996, p 55).
And it is to Jesus' meals that we must go back if we want to recapture
the fulness of meaning of the Last Supper and of the Eucharist, and
face their challenge. The Eucharist is the sacrament of Jesus' Passover,
of Jesus' sacrifice, beyond any doubt. But it is also a *meal.* And Jesus'
table-companionship will be the angle from which we will reflect on
the Eucharist.

CHAPTER TWO

The Role of Meals in Jesus' Ministry

It would be interesting and instructive if, before reading the following reflections, you, the reader, would take time to go through the gospels, and assess the place of meals in Jesus' ministry: if you are alone, it will be enough to take one gospel, for instance Matthew, or Luke; if you can work with a group, you could divide the gospels between the members of the group.

What should you be looking for? Do not aim at reading thoroughly each gospel; it would take too much time, and it is not necessary at this stage. Rather, leaf attentively through the gospel you have chosen, focusing your attention, (i) on the meals Jesus shared with people; (ii) on meals and banquets used by Jesus as symbols of the Kingdom; (iii) on reflections made by people about Jesus as a table-companion. Note down your findings as you progress through the text, not forgetting the exact references of the texts you find relevant.

Once you have finished your investigation, try to answer the following questions: what is it that strikes you concerning the place of meals in the gospels – the mentality, the style, and the approach of Jesus to people? If you are working with a group, you could share your answers to these questions with one another.

Impressions of Jesus as a Table-Companion

'In reading the gospels, we might be forgiven for thinking that Jesus is always coming from, going to, or talking about banquets, feasts and meals. He is remembered vividly as a companion at table, and as someone to whom meals were very important. Opponents coined a catch-call and flung it at him: 'Look, a glutton and a drunkard, a friend of tax-collectors and sinners' (Eamonn Bredin, *Disturbing the Peace*, Columba Press, 1985, Dublin, p 134).

Leafing through the gospels, we notice the importance of meals in Jesus' experience, and in his teaching; the four Gospels agree on this. We find Jesus sharing meals with people, speaking about meals, during his ministry in Galilee, but also during his ministry in Jerusalem. Actually, the gospels show us Jesus' as table-companion, not only during his ministry, but also after his resurrection.

We must therefore say that there is hardly any exaggeration in Eamonn Bredin's remark: meals were very important to Jesus, and they constitute an essential experience in the Gospels, if we want to understand Jesus, his ministry, the Kingdom, the God whom Jesus had come to reveal to the world.

Jesus' Table-Companions

The most striking thing about Jesus' table companionship is that he shared meals with all sorts of people: with Pharisees who invited him (Lk 7:36ff; 14:1); with his friends at Bethany (Lk 10:38-42); with tax-collectors (Mk 2:15-17); and especially, it seems, with people labelled 'sinners'; and it was that which drew criticism from the Pharisees.

What was for Jesus the meaning, the role of these meals in his ministry, in the mission which had been entrusted to him by the Father? Why did Jesus share meals with 'tax-collectors and sinners'? John the Baptist, Jesus' Precursor, and his teacher, had been so different: 'he came, neither eating nor drinking' (Mt 11:18), and if he did meet sinners, he invited them to repent and to be baptised (see Mt 3:1-12), not to share a meal with him.

To the scribes of the Pharisee party who objected to his attitude, Jesus seemed to suggest that to him, table companionship was meant to be, for sinners, a 'healing experience' (Mk 2:16-17). In order to understand Jesus' answer, we will have to see Jesus' open table companionship within the context of the Judaism of his time.

At this stage of our reflection, what can we conclude? In their story of the institution of the Eucharist by Jesus during the Last Supper, both Luke and Paul (I Cor 11:24-25; Lk 22:19-20) conclude Jesus' words over the bread and the wine with the invitation: 'Do this in memory of me.' We will reflect later on the 'programme' which these words set for us. Just now, could we simply listen to them and receive them from Jesus who 'welcomed sinners and ate with them.' What could these words mean in my own life now, in my relationship with people, at home, in my community? Could not this be one of the demands made on me by the celebration of the Eucharist?

Jesus' Table-Companionship in the Context of the Judaism of his time

When the Pharisees objected to Jesus sharing meals with tax collectors and sinners, it was obviously in the name of Jewish Tradition. What then was the practice of table-companionship in Jesus' Jewish society?

Meals as Covenant Experiences

The biblical key to the understanding of Israel's history, life and thought is surely the Covenant: that is, the bond by which God bound to himself the people he had brought out of Egypt, the land of slavery. The Covenant is the very foundation of Israel's identity: 'You will be my people, I will be your God' (Ex 19:5-6).

The covenant-bond which bound the Israelites to God and to one another was meant to inspire their whole life; not just their prayer, or their sacrifices. And therefore, the covenant law aimed at making the Israelites' daily life a covenant life. And that was true especially of meals. For meals were 'covenant experiences.'

Practising Jews at the time of Jesus, just as today, considered meals, – especially festive meals – as sacred experiences: meals commemorated, made present in some way, the Covenant bond; they expressed this bond in a unique manner. Sharing a common meal meant sharing the fruit of the land given by God to his people, and therefore it both expressed and strengthened the communion which the Covenant created between them.

It was this 'theological dimension' of meals which gave the many rules regulating meals their religious character: far from seeing them as a burden, religious Jews accepted them as expressions of their faith in God, the Holy God, the Covenant God.

Concretely, what did this holiness demand of Jews sharing a meal together? It demanded, for instance, that before sitting at table for a meal, guests would purify their hands. The *Talmud* (a collection of Jewish rabbinical literature) counts as many as 600 precepts on the purification of hands; Jesus had difficulties with the Pharisees on this: 'The Pharisees and some of the scribes who had come from Jerusalem gathered round him, and they noticed that some of his disciples were eating with unclean hands, that is, without washing them... So the Pharisees and scribes asked him, "why do your disciples not respect the tradition of the elders but eat their food with unclean hands"' (Mk 7:3-4).

Utensils used to prepare meals had also to be purified. As for food, its choice was of the greatest importance: one should read the food regulations of Leviticus (chapter 11) to understand how far reaching, in daily life, was the ideal of 'holiness' to which the Covenant called the people of Israel.

And these regulations were no light matter: remember Peter's reaction when, after Pentecost, being invited, in a vision, to eat the meal of animals considered 'unclean' by the law, he immediately answered: 'Certainly not, Lord, I have never yet eaten anything profane or unclean' (Acts 10:11-14).

If so much care was taken when preparing meals, or preparing for meals, we can easily understand how selective hosts were when it came to inviting people who would sit at table with them. According to the Babylonian *Talmud*, people with a pure conscience would never accept an invitation to a meal, unless they knew who the other guests were. The reason behind this attitude was that if one was not careful, one would run the risk of sharing a meal with someone who was not ritually 'pure'; the presence of such a person would, in some way, contaminate the other guests.

We are therefore entitled to conclude that in Jesus' society, meals, especially festive meals, were moments of communion for the just in the covenant community, moments of communion for the in-group. And consequently, moments of separation, of discrimination against outsiders.

And it is against this background that we must evaluate both Jesus' attitude to people in matters of table-fellowship, and the Pharisees' reaction to this attitude.

'This man welcomes sinners and eats with them' (Luke 15:2)

As an introduction to three parables in which Jesus tells us about God's immense mercy (the parables of the lost sheep, of the lost coin, and of the lost son), Luke quotes a reflection made by Pharisees and scribes who were shocked by Jesus' attitude: 'This man, they said, welcomes sinners and eats with them' (Lk 15:2). These few words sum up the opinion Pharisees and scribes had of Jesus.

But why did Jesus insist on sharing meals with people labelled 'sinners', whom good practising Jews avoided? Why was he not content with speaking with them, inviting them to repent? It would have been so much simpler, and in that way, Jesus would not have scandalised anyone.

In order to enter into Jesus' mind on this question, let us go back to a story we have already alluded to: the story of a meal to which Jesus was invited, together with his disciples, and which he shared with 'tax-collectors and sinners.' We take this story from Mark's Gospel (2:15-17; see also Matthew 9:10-13, and Luke 5:29-32).

'As Jesus sat at dinner in Levi's house, many tax collectors and sinners were also sitting with Jesus and his disciples – for there were many who followed him. When the scribes of the Pharisees saw that he was eating with sinners and tax collectors, they said to his disciples: "Why does he eat with tax collectors and sinners"? When Jesus heard this, he said to them, "Those who are well have no need of a physician, but those who are sick; I have come to call not the righteous but sinners"' (Mk 2:13-17).

Let us look at this story: it is the story of a controversy between scribes of the Pharisee party and Jesus, and the object of the controversy is Jesus' sharing a meal with tax-collectors and sinners: 'Why does he eat with tax collectors and sinners?' (Mk 2:16).

Can we identify with sufficient precision who were the 'tax collectors and sinners' whose presence was unacceptable at the table of 'the just'?

We know what sort of people tax-collectors were; they collaborated with the Romans, and as such were unclean and considered as traitors; they also had the reputation of being dishonest (see the story of Zacchaeus in Luke 19:1-10).

But what about sinners? The Pharisees would have easily called 'sinners' people who lived outside the boundaries of their group; people who did not know the law; and did not go out of their way to learn and observe it in all its details: 'this rabble knows nothing about the law, they are damned' (John 7:49); (see James D. G. Dunn, *Jesus, Paul and the Law*, SPCK, London 1990, pp 72,75).

But the label, 'sinners', also covered 'professional sinners' such as usurers, and prostitutes. They, more anybody else, were 'excommunicated' from the table-fellowship of 'the just.'

When Jesus had met John the Baptist near the Jordan river, he had already identified with the sinners who came to John to be baptized; sitting at table with sinners, he expressed his own understanding of his mission: he had come, not to usher in God's anger, not to crush sinners, but in God's name, to enter into communion with them.

Not just 'being with', but 'eating with…'

The vocabulary of the story in Mark 2:15-17 is very suggestive on this point: the scribes of the Pharisee party objected to Jesus *not* because 'he was with sinners', but because 'he sat at table with them', 'he ate with them.' Hence the catch-call which his opponents flung at him, 'A glutton and a drunkard, a friend of tax-collectors and sinners' (Mt 11:19); 'This man welcomes sinners and eats with them' (Lk 15:2).

That is, within the Jewish context of his time, Jesus was criticized, attacked, because he not only accepted, but sought to share with sinners a 'covenant experience', to share with them the fruit of the covenant land.

What did Jesus seek to achieve through table-companionship with people religious minded Jews tended to marginalise?

We can take it for granted that Jesus' attitude was not determined simply by sociological reasons: he did not simply want to bring back sinners into the main stream of society; though, obviously, that too was important; and actually, Jesus' attitude to marginals may have at least opened the road leading back to their re-insertion into the community.

Table-Companionship as Healing

But Jesus had come to reveal God, to translate into human terms God's infinite kindness and mercy.

Again here, Mark's story is very expressive: 'The scribes of the Pharisees said to his disciples, Why does he eat with tax-collectors and sinners? When Jesus heard this he said to them, 'It is not the healthy who need the doctor but the sick' (Mk 2:17).

Thus, to Jesus, the table-fellowship which he offered to sinners was meant to be, for them, a healing experience. In what way? Marginalised as they were by Jewish society, or at least by groups in Jewish society, sinners must have felt respected, accepted, welcomed, loved by Jesus who responded to their invitations, or invited them without any preconditions. And Jesus' attitude to them was not just a show – they felt he loved them.

We can easily imagine the impression Jesus must have made on prostitutes when they heard him say to the high priests and elders: 'I tell you solemnly, tax collectors and prostitutes are making their way into the kingdom of God before you' (J. Jeremias, *New Testament Theology II*, p 117, translates, 'they are making their way into the kingdom, not you', Mt 21:31).

And Jesus was not just a kind person going out of his way to show respect to unloved people: the men and women with whom he shared meals knew he was also someone who spoke with authority, unlike the scribes, as if his words sprung out of his own experience of God. It was God himself who through Jesus reached out to them. Through Jesus, sharing meals with tax collectors and sinners, God, – the God whom Jesus called 'Abba' – became reality in the lives of those people.

And thus began the community of the Kingdom: the table-companionship that Jesus offered to sinners, to marginals, did not suppress the boundaries which Jewish society, and especially groups such as the Pharisees, had established around themselves, to protect themselves, to affirm their difference. When tax collectors and sinners went back home after having shared a meal with Jesus, their neighbours still considered them as 'unclean people' to be avoided. But now, sinners knew that there was a community to which they could go back, where they knew they would always be welcomed, the community developing around Jesus.

Healing as a Journey

The meals they shared with Jesus were, for sinners, an experience of respect, acceptance, communion; Jesus called it an experience of 'healing.' But healing is a process, it takes time. The community that grew around Jesus was not a community of 'perfect people', but rather of 'people on their way.'

Concretely, that meant that the men and women who had met Jesus and shared meals with him had begun the long and difficult journey of their conversion. Instant, total, conversion looks good in books, it does not correspond to reality.

Theologians have asked themselves what was special in the forgiveness Jesus offered to people through table-fellowship. I like the way Sanders puts it: 'while everyone said, God forgives you *if* you will repent and mend your ways, Jesus said, God forgives you, *and now,* you should repent and mend your ways' (E. P. Sanders, *Jesus and Judaism*, SPCK, London, 1985, p 204). That might be a good way of putting it: Jesus' table-fellowship was, so to speak, the 'sacrament' of God's forgiveness offered in and through Jesus; a sacrament which was the joyful, deeply loving and human celebration of salvation from God; of healing in the making. Through this 'sacrament', people felt invited to start their journey; or, in the words of Joachim Jeremias, 'to start learning how to say Abba to God.'

The gospels are not just meant to tell us about the Jesus of 2,000 years ago. They are the call of the Risen Lord addressed to the Church today. In this sense, Jesus' words at the Last Supper, 'Do this in memory of me', can be understood as referring, not just to the Eucharistic Ritual, but also to the whole of Jesus' mission.

'Do this in memory of me': 'This man welcomes sinners and eats with them'! So should we!

CHAPTER THREE

The Kingdom of God is like a Banquet

'This man welcomes sinners and eats with them '(Lk 15:2). As we have seen, Jesus was in the habit of sharing meals with people whom Jewish society pushed out to the margin, people like tax-collectors, and sinners. As Luke puts it, through sharing meals with them, Jesus welcomed them, offered them to enter into an experience of communion with him and with one another. Through table-fellowship, Jesus made the Kingdom begin to become a reality in the life of those people. For the Kingdom, God's Kingdom, Abba's Kingdom is communion; it is Abba's dream to see his children 'come from east and west and sit down with Abraham, and Isaac and Jacob at the feast in the Kingdom of Heaven' (see Mt 8:11) – a feast which is symbolized, quite naturally, by a banquet.

There is one parable of Jesus which expresses this beautifully: the parable of 'the invited guests.' We have two versions of it: one in Matthew 22:1-14; the other in Luke 14:15-24.

But before we take up this parable, let us examine briefly its context in the religious experience of God's People in the Old Testament.

The Old Testament Context

Meals play a very important part in human experience; not simply because eating is vital, literally; but also because meals, when shared with people, can create, or express a bond between table-companions.

Quite naturally, therefore, meals, banquets will be used in order to express, to strengthen the at-oneness of a religious group: at-oneness between the members of the group, at-oneness between the group and the divinity. And thus, sacred meals were part of Israel's religious experience. There was actually a category of sacrifice, which was widespread in the semitic world and beyond, which was called 'communion sacrifice' (see Leviticus 3): a family, a group would buy an animal to be offered in sacrifice; part of the animal would be burnt on the altar, and thus made over to God; but one portion of the victim was eaten at a sacred banquet. 'It seems to have been the most commonly celebrated sacrifice in ancient Israel and the central rite of her feasts. Since it was a meal 'shared' with God, it expressed, better than any other sacrifice, the union of God with God's faithful' (see Jerusalem Bible, Lv 3:1). It was a joyful celebration: These (your offerings) you shall eat in the presence of the *Lord* your God at the place that the *Lord* your God will choose, you together with your son and your daughter, your male and female slaves, and the Levites resident in your towns, rejoicing in the presence of the *Lord* your God in all your undertakings' (Deut 12:18).

The Book of Deuteronomy gives great importance to meals and to the link between meals and worship (see Deut 12); but the celebration in words, song and dance takes priority over the material aspects of a banquet. What matters most is not the food that is eaten, or the way it is prepared, but being together, celebrating together.

We can now easily understand why the Old Testament prophets, when they wanted to express the beauty, the richness of the Messianic times, had recourse, quite naturally, to the communion experience of meals and banquets: 'On this mountain, for all peoples, the Lord of hosts is preparing a banquet of rich food, a banquet of fine wines, of succulent food, of well-strained wines. On this mountain, he has destroyed the veil which used to veil all peoples, the pall enveloping all nations; he has destroyed death for ever. The Lord God has wiped away the tears from every cheek; he has taken his people's shame away everywhere on earth, for the Lord has spoken' (Isaiah 25:6-8).

In this text from Isaiah, one will note where the prophet seems to put the stress: the banquet prepared by God will be offered to all peoples.

It is interesting to note also how rabbinic tradition tended to comment on such texts: the banquet theme was developed in the period between the first and the second 'Testaments', and it was understood as referring to the 'messianic times.' But somehow, the idea that the gentiles would be invited to take part in the banquet, was toned down. The Targum (an Aramaic version of the Scriptures which comments as much as it translates) paraphrases Isaiah 25:6 as follows: 'The Lord of hosts will make for all the peoples in this mountain a meal; and though they suppose it is an honour, it will be a shame for them, and great plagues from which they will be unable to escape, plagues whereby they will come to their end.' Clearly, in this commentary, the vision of Isaiah has vanished (see Kenneth E. Bailey, *Through Peasant Eyes*, Eerdmans, Grand Rapids, Michigan, 1980, p 90).

The Qumran community (a Jewish monastic community at the time of Jesus) was animated by the same spirit: in a text of the community, called the 'Messianic Rule', we read of how, in the last days, the Messiah will gather with the whole congregation to eat bread and drink wine. But the 'congregation' has very clearly defined frontiers: no one is allowed in who is 'smitten in his flesh, or paralyzed in his feet or hands, or lame, or blind, or deaf, or dumb, or smitten in his flesh with a visible blemish.'

All gentiles are obviously excluded and, along with them, all imperfect Jews. Again here, Isaiah's open-ended vision has been blurred if not eliminated (Kenneth E. Bailey, ibid p 90-91).

Thus, in Old Testament times, on the one hand, common meals, banquets, could, through their very nature, symbolize the religious experience of communion with God, and with the members of a religious group; a communion which the prophets saw as offered to all peoples. But just as meals can become, in our human experience, moments of exclusion, of discrimination, of apartheid, in the same way, a sacred meal could easily become the privilege of those who saw themselves as 'the just', as truly belonging to the community, to the exclusion of others. There seems to be in us sinful human beings, an instinct which leads us to seek to manipulate everyone, everything, including sacred things, including God, so as to make them our own to the exclusion of 'others' – and that, so often, in God's name.

'The Kingdom of God is like a Banquet...'

Before we reflect on Jesus' parable of the Banquet, we must remember, once again, what meals were, in Jesus' experience: moments of welcome, of healing, of communion offered especially to those on the margins of society: 'This man welcomes sinners and eats with them' (Lk 15:2).

The Jesus of the Parables is obviously the same Jesus; and the parables of the Banquet in the Kingdom will have to be understood in the light of Jesus' ministry. We could add even now that the parables of the Banquet, in their turn, will throw light on the meaning and impact of Jesus' meals.

The Parable of the Invited Guests (Luke 14:15-24)

We have good reasons to believe that Luke was of Greek, pagan origin, and that after he had become a Christian, he accompanied Paul at least on some of his missionary journeys. As a missionary, Luke witnessed how, on the one hand, pagans flocked into the Christian communities in Syria, Asia Minor, Greece, and even in Rome; while, on the other hand, most of the Jews, the members of God's chosen people, stayed away; or, if they did become Christians, found it difficult to live with converts from paganism. The parable of The Invited Guests in Luke chapter 14 echoes this experience of Luke the missionary.

The Context of the Parable in Luke's Gospel

There seems to be two major themes in this chapter: the first part (14:1-24) offers sayings of Jesus connected with meals. The second part (14:25-35) is focused on 'renouncing possessions.'

In the following chapter, Luke has grouped three parables, called 'parables of mercy' which are presented as Jesus' answer to a criticism directed at him by Pharisees and scribes: 'This man welcomes sinners and eats with them.'

Let us have now a closer look at Luke 14:7-14, that is, the part of chapter 14 which immediately precedes the parable of The Invited Guests: it is a story about choosing places at table (Lk 14:7-11). Note what Jesus has to say about the attitude of people invited to a meal:

they should behave humbly, and not like people who want to lord it over others.

In the next story, 'on choosing guests to be invited' (Lk 14:12-14), Jesus insists that one should invite especially people who cannot repay, 'the poor, the crippled, the lame, the blind' (14:13). This story is particularly important since it comes immediately before the parable on which we are going to reflect.

Thus the context of Luke's parable of the Invited Guests seems to give us an image of God as a host whose tastes, and manners are strange, so different from our own – the image of a God who has revealed himself in, and through Jesus, especially the Jesus who shared so many meals with those on the margins, with sinners.

The text of Luke's Parable of the Invited Guests (Luke 14:15-24)

As we read this parable, we focus our attention first on the host who has prepared a banquet for his guests; he is obviously at the centre of the parable; it is on him that Jesus wants to focus. His aim is clearly to have his banquet hall filled to capacity (14:23).

Let us now look at the guests: there are three groups. Without pushing too far, one can see a historical parallel between the first group to be invited and the people of Israel (Lk 14:16-20); between the second group within the city walls (the poor, the crippled, the blind, the lame) and the Jewish tax-collectors and sinners (Lk 14:21); and between those outside the city walls and the Gentiles (Lk 14:22-23).

We note how the text presents each group: the guests who were first invited, but refused to come (14:15-20); the poor, the crippled, the blind and the lame found in the streets and alleys of the town (14:21); and finally people found outside the town, on the open roads and the hedgerows (14:23). Even if the main point of the parable is not the kind of people who eventually take part in the banquet, who they are is not totally irrelevant: Jesus met every day people like that in his ministry.

Finally, it is clear that no special conditions of admission to the banquet are imposed on the people found 'in the streets and alleys of the town (14:21), or 'on the open roads and the hedgerows' (14:23).

The Message

As we have already pointed out, the parable of 'the Invited Guests' in Luke's gospel probably reflects Luke's experience as a missionary, as one of Paul's companions: while Luke rejoiced at the massive conversion of pagans to Christianity, he must have been struck, and pained, by the demands made by a number of Jewish Christians on converts from paganism: not only should they accept circumcision (Acts 15:1), but they should also observe the law of Moses, especially the rules concerning meals.

Luke himself, like Paul, could not see any reason to demand from pagans coming to Christianity, anything else but faith in Christ the Saviour. He wanted Christian communities to be wide open; and in this, Luke, like Paul, echoed Jesus' attitude: 'This man welcomes sinners and eats with them' (Lk 15:2). Obviously, in welcoming sinners, Jesus took risks. But he took them in the name of the kindness and mercy of his Father whose heart and hands he was in the world.

We thus have, in Luke's parable, an extraordinary statement made about the God of the Kingdom revealed by Jesus: a God who 'has prepared a great banquet…for a large number of people.' A God who does not ex-communicate anyone: if there are guests who are 'excommunicated', it is not the host's decision, but theirs. A God who does not show himself selective concerning the guests who do come to the banquet: he does not impose on them any pre-condition; and therefore, he takes the risk that some might not be suited for the Kingdom. A gracious God 'who takes delight in throwing a banquet…, a God who wants the company of others, and who is not unaffected when the guests refuse to come and feast with him…. A God who is hungry for table-company, a God who will not sit down at table and start the banquet until all the places have been filled' (Denis McBride, *The Gospel of Luke*, Dominican Publications, Dublin 1991, p 195).

This is the God of Jesus. The God Jesus invites us to celebrate and proclaim, 'Do this in memory of me.'

The Parable of the Wedding Feast (Matthew 22:1-14)

The God revealed by Jesus in the parable of the Invited Guests, as we found it in Luke's gospel (14:15-24) resembles the God of the parable of the Prodigal Son (Lk 15:11-32): the prodigal son is not asked to put on a 'wedding garment' before he enters his father's home; the father gives it to him (15:22). Does the parable of the Wedding Feast in Matthew's gospel offer the same message?

Early Christianity through Judaeo-Christian Eyes

Before we take up Matthew's parable, we must remember that Matthew's gospel seems to express a catechesis for Christian communities in which many Christians were of Jewish origin, and therefore converts from Judaism. These Christians obviously acknowledged Jesus as Christ and Lord, and Saviour. At the same time, they remained deeply attached to what they saw as the major values of Judaism: the Law of Moses; circumcision as the initiation rite into the covenant community; the purity rules concerning food; concerning relationships with pagans.

One should read the first fifteen chapters in the Acts of the Apostles to see the difficulties which Christians coming from Judaism had in accepting that Christians coming from paganism should not be forced, for instance, to submit to the Jewish regulations concerning 'the clean and unclean' (see Acts 10). To them, it was a matter of faith. It will be interesting to see how far Matthew's parable of the Wedding Banquet addresses the mentality of Jewish Christians in the first century a.d., and what its meaning can be for us today.

The Context of the Parable in Matthew's Gospel (Matthew 21:1-22:14)

The brunt of nearly all the stories in Matthew 21, the chapter which immediately precedes the Parable of the Wedding Feast, is that the leaders of God's chosen people are no longer fit to fulfill their mission. They may be 'the guests of the parable who were the first to be invited', but their attitude expresses their refusal to go to the banquet.

As to why Matthew shows himself so negative concerning his people, we must remember that when the final redactor of the first gospel was putting the finishing touches to his book, it was evident, on the one hand, that Israel as a whole, had not accepted Jesus of Nazareth as the Messiah; and on the other hand, Jerusalem had been destroyed in 70 a.d., by the Romans; there was no longer any temple. It will take time for the Pharisees to save Judaism from utter ruin. Matthew's pessimism must be understood in the light of all these events. In all likelihood, the parable of the Wedding Feast will reflect the same spirit as the parables which precede it.

The Parable of the Wedding Feast

At first sight, we note that if Matthew's and Luke's texts differ in structure and detail, their content and message are basically the same: the host who has prepared the banquet wants the banquet hall to be filled to capacity (compare Lk 14:23 and Mt 22:30).

But we note above all that, to the parable of the Banquet which he has in common with Luke (Mt 22:1-10), Matthew has added a second parable, that of the Wedding Garment (22:11-14). Why? We will come back to that later.

The Parable of the Banquet (Matthew 14:1-10)

Let us first focus our attention on the host in the parable of the wedding banquet: who is he? Luke said simply 'a man'; Matthew says, 'a king who gave a feast for his son's wedding.' Thus Matthew gives his parable, from the beginning, a 'messianic turn' (the royal messiah!); and from the beginning too, he prepares the introduction of his second parable, that of the Wedding Garment.

Who are the guests? Matthew distinguishes three successive invitations: the first two invitations (22:1-10) are addressed to people who were in some way expected to take part in the feast: they, at first, refuse (we could think of the prophets' call in the OT); they also refuse a second call (perhaps that of Jesus' apostles?) and even go as far as killing the servants sent to invite them (the first Christian martyrs?).

In the background, we must see, in all likelihood, the experience of the Christian mission among the Jews, the first persecutions directed against Christians, and the ruin of Jerusalem in 70 A.D.; ruin which Matthew sees as a punishment inflicted by God to guests who had been invited and behaved in an odious manner (Mt 22:5-7).

The third invitation (22:8-10) probably represents the beginning of the Christian mission to the pagan world: the servants go out 'onto the roads' and invite everyone they could find, 'bad and good alike' (22:9-10), and no conditions of any sort seem to be imposed on them:

'invited', they go and take place in the wedding hall.

The 'provisional conclusion' which Matthew gives to the parable of the Wedding Feast resembles that of Luke's parable in the sense that the aim the host had in view is clearly attained: '...and the wedding hall was filled with guests' (Mt 22:10).

The Parable of 'the Wedding Garment' (Matthew 22:11-14)

The parable of the Wedding Garment seems to follow the first parable quite naturally: 'When the King came to look at the guests he noticed one man...' (22:11). Actually, Matthew announced the shorter parable as early as 22:2 when he presented the banquet prepared by the king as a 'wedding banquet.'

At the same time, however, we note the lack of harmony between the shorter parable and the parable of the Wedding Feast: how could one demand of people found 'on the roads' that they be equipped with a wedding garment. It has been suggested that, actually, the custom was to offer festal clothing to guests as they entered the banquet hall. But there is no evidence for such custom at the time of Jesus; and Matthew does not say anything about that; and yet, it was a very important point to make (see Edward Schweizer, *The Good News According to Matthew*, SPCK, London 1980, p 416-417).

Again, note the contrast between the conclusion of 22:14 ('many are called but few are chosen') and the picture one is given of the banquet hall in 22:10b: 'the wedding hall was filled with guests', and only one of the guests was expelled.

Finally, is there not some contradiction between the attitude of the king of the first parable who, in his generosity and openness, wants the wedding hall filled to capacity and the king of the second parable who comes in to look at the guests and wants to check on their identity?

How then did Matthew himself understand the parable of the Wedding Garment?

The Message of the Parable in Matthew's Gospel

We have already noted that the parable of 'the Uninvited Guests' in Luke's gospel echoed in some way the experience of Luke the missionary who marvelled at the number of pagans flocking to the Christian communities founded by Paul. Jesus, now the Risen Lord, truly continued to be present and active through his messengers, through them he invited generously 'the poor and maimed and blind and lame', wherever they could be, in the streets and lanes of the city, or in the highways or hedges: 'that my house may be filled' (Lk 14:23). It was a risky affair: people might be let into the banquet hall who actually should not be admitted. But Jesus of Nazareth did not seem to be afraid of this risk, as is shown, for instance, by the parable of the Prodigal Son (Lk 15:11-32).

Actually, the host, in Luke's parable, is so keen on sharing the meal he has prepared with as many guests as possible that he asks his servants 'to compel people to come in': an expression which could easily be misunderstood, but which, within the context of the ancient Middle East, shows, on the contrary, the loving attention of the host: 'In the Middle East, the unexpected invitation must be refused. The refusal is all the more required if the guest is of lower social rank than the host: the offer is generous and delightful, but (thinks the stranger) the host cannot possibly mean it. After some discussion the servant will finally have to take the startled guest by the arm and gently pull him along. There is no other way to convince him that he is really invited to the great banquet, irrespective of his being a foreigner. Grace is unbelievable!' (Kenneth E. Bailey, *Through Peasant Eyes*, Eerdmans, Grand Rapids, Michigan, 1980, p 108-109).

God's unbelievable merciful love revealed by Jesus, the Jesus of table-companionship, the Jesus of the Parable of the Banquet! The Jesus who never tires of telling us, 'Do this in memory of me.'

The Message of the Parable of the Wedding Garment

With the parable of 'the Wedding Garment', the relationship between the host and his guests seems to undergo a major, and rather frightening change: the generous host, willing to take risks so as to have the banquet hall filled to capacity, has become an austere and severe judge who does not hesitate to have one of the guests expelled because he did not wear a wedding garment. The contrast between the two parables is difficult to understand.

Actually, scholars consider the parable of 'the Wedding Garment' as being, originally, an independent parable, and it was not joined to the parable of the banquet from the outset; its theme is that of the Last Judgement: the time of salvation has come, and it will be missed by anyone who does not prepare himself/herself (see Ed Schweizer, op. cit, p 417).

But why did Matthew, or his source, bring the two parables together? The history of the development of the early Church, as we find it outlined by Luke in the Acts of the Apostles, will perhaps help us to understand Matthew's concern.

Christianity had begun as a 'marginal group' in Judaism; and it took time before it grew into an independent movement. Actually, as we read the Acts of the Apostles, we are struck by the fact that the disciples, even after Pentecost, continued to go to the Temple in Jerusalem, to pray there (Acts 3:1); they felt at home within the institutions of Judaism. And the first Christians, of Jewish origin, continued to observe the Jewish law, especially the laws concerning food, and table-fellowship (Acts 10:9-16; 11,1-3).

When pagans began to ask for admission into the Judaeo-Christian communities, they had, of course, to embrace faith in Christ the Saviour; but they were also asked to conform to the laws and customs of Judaism. In other words, pagans were asked to put on, so to speak, the wedding garment of Judaism. To the Judaeo-Christians, it was the obvious thing to do. But was it?

In 49 A.D., the leaders of the Church met in Jerusalem to reflect precisely on the question of pagans who had become Christians: how far should they be asked to comply with the Law of Moses? The final decision of the 'council', at least according to Luke (but not according to Paul, see Galatians 2:1-10)), was the result of a compromise between the more conservative Judaeo-Christian approach, defended by James, and the more open and liberal approach of the missionaries like Paul and Barnabas; it showed that the Judaeo-Christians were willing to be welcoming towards pagan converts, but at the same time, it did show how difficult it was for Judaeo-Christians to distinguish between culture and faith (see Acts 15:22-29). The apostles and the elders, with the consent of the whole church, decided to choose men from among their members and to send them to Antioch with Paul and Barnabas…, with the following letter: '… It has seemed good to the Holy Spirit and to us to impose on you no further burden than these essentials: that you abstain from what has been sacrificed to idols and from blood and from what is strangled and from fornication. If you keep yourselves from these, you will do well. Farewell' (Acts 15:22-29).

It is important to note that Paul gives us, in his letter to the Galatians, a different version of the Jerusalem meeting, and of its final decision: 'when James and Cephas and John, who were acknowledged pillars, recognized the grace that had been given to me, they gave to Barnabas and me the right hand of fellowship, agreeing that we should go to the Gentiles and they to the circumcised. They asked only one thing, that we remember the poor, which was actually what I was eager to do (Gal 2:9-10).

In other words, the leaders of the early Church did not all always think in the same way, and did not always agree on the policy they had to follow; and this, in matters which were not unimportant. It may be that Paul's attitude and pastoral practice made it more difficult for the Jews to join Christian communities, and for Judaeo-Christians to live in harmony with converts from paganism. But Paul certainly contributed powerfully to the spread of the gospel in Asia Minor, in Greece, and as far as Rome.

Let us now come back to Matthew's twin parable of the 'Wedding Banquet' and of the 'Wedding Garment.' It is perhaps within this context of the development of the early Church as we have just outlined it, that Matthew's message can be best understood.

The parable of the Wedding Garment reassured the Judaeo-Christians who lived in communities in which there were a significant and growing number of converts from paganism: yes, these converts must be welcomed; they have been brought in by 'the king's servants on the king's orders', without any precondition. But that did not mean that their way and style of life was immaterial: they had to wear a wedding garment; that is, in the words of the letter sent to Antioch by the 'Jerusalem council', they had 'to abstain from what has been sacrificed to idols and from blood and from what is strangled and from fornication' (Acts 15:28-29).

As we have already noted, Paul put it much more simply, in a way which was fully consonant with the Gospel, 'They asked only one thing, that we remember the poor, which was actually what I was eager to do' (Gal 2:10).

Matthew's approach was that of a pastor who wanted to help all the members of the communities he ministered to, to feel truly at home in the Christian fold. One may wonder how Christians coming from paganism understood and accepted his efforts. In his book on Jesus and Judaism, E. P. Sanders notes that 'a high tolerance for sinners was not a characteristic of the early Church, as far as we can know it.' As far as we ourselves are concerned today, we must probably say that the Church's attitude, over the centuries, has been more Matthaean than Lukan: the wedding garment to be worn at the table of the Kingdom, has tended to become 'a whole wardrobe' and thus a very great number of people have been, and are still being kept away from the healing experience which the Lord's Supper is meant to be. We must untiringly go back to the gospels and let Jesus teach us again and again 'to welcome sinners and eat with them'.

CHAPTER FOUR

Jesus' Last Meal with his Disciples

The last hours Jesus spent with his disciples before he died, were in the context of a meal. The early Christian communities soon saw in the Last Supper a major event in Jesus' life and mission; all the more as it soon became in the Christian communities, the heart of a celebration in which it was 'remembered', 'commemorated', 'made present': it became known as the Lord's Supper, the Breaking of Bread.

Then theology, spirituality, Christian art focused on it; and after twenty centuries of reflection, meditation and celebration, we are still investigating its riches. Our reflections, here, will focus on the Last Supper as a meal.

A Glance at the Texts

The texts are many. Not only do we find an account of the Last Supper in each one of the four gospels, but also in Paul's first letter to the Corinthians. And we must add to these the 'Discourse on the Bread of Life' in John chapter 6.

But all these texts do not approach the Last Supper in the same way. There is, first, the very short, austere account of Paul in I Cor II. Paul's is the most ancient account of all (around 57 A.D.); it is inserted in a warning given by Paul to the Christians of Corinth concerning the way the celebration of the Lord's Supper had developed in their community. And in order to help them recapture the original meaning of the celebration, Paul in three verses (11:23-25), tells them the story of Jesus' Last Meal: 'For I received from the Lord what I also handed on to you, that the Lord Jesus, on the night when he was betrayed took a loaf of bread, and when he had given thanks, he broke it and said: "This is my body that is for you. Do this in memory of me." In the same way he took the cup also, after supper, saying, "This cup is the new covenant in my blood. Do this, as often as you drink it, in memory of me. For as often as you eat this bread and drink this cup, you proclaim the Lord's death until he comes"' (I Cor 11:23-26).

Mark (dated c. 70 a.d.), Matthew and Luke (both dated c. 80-90 A.D.) give us slightly more developed accounts – Mk 14:17-23, Mt 26-30-35, Lk 22:31-34. Yet, neither Mark, Matthew nor Luke, go much beyond the 'ritual' story, as it must have been shaped very early for the 'liturgical celebrations' of the first Christian communities. It would be impossible to recapture, from Mark's or Matthew's accounts, the emotion or feelings of Jesus and his disciples as they shared their last meal.

John's story (around 100-110 A.D.) is by far the longest: he has five chapters (chs 13-17) on the Last Supper. John does not say a word about the institution of the Eucharist; instead, he dwells at length on the relationship that must bind the disciples together in the love with which the Father in and though Jesus embraces them.

We certainly cannot consider these texts as detailed, accurate accounts of the Last Supper. As we have already pointed out, Mark's, Matthew's and Luke's story, together with Paul's, are very much 'stereotyped': they look like 'liturgical texts', marked therefore by the austerity, and a certain reticence.

The Last Supper and the Jewish Passover

Let us begin with a few words about the immediate context in which Jesus took his last meal with his disciples.

There is no agreement among the gospels as to the nature of Jesus' last meal: Mark, Matthew and Luke present it as the Jewish Passover meal which opened the celebration of the Jewish Passover: 'The disciples set out and went to the city, and found everything as he had told them; and they prepared the Passover meal (Mk 14:12,16; Mt 26:17-19; Lk 22:7-13).

But in giving us the story of the meal itself, they hardly refer to the Passover ritual. As if that was, to them, of little importance for the understanding of the meal.

John, on the contrary, states explicitly that it was on the evening of the day that Jesus died, (we would say, on Friday) that the Jews ate the Passover meal (Jn 19:31). But he does set firmly Jesus' last meal within the context of the Jewish Passover: 'Before the festival of the Passover, Jesus, knowing that his hour had come to pass from this world to the Father, having loved those who were his in the world, loved them to the end' (Jn 13:1).

The Jewish Passover meal was meant to celebrate, to commemorate the great night of Israel's 'liberation': 'I am the Lord your God who brought you out of Egypt, out of the house of bondage' (Ex 20:1).

We could say, therefore, that Jesus and his disciples, as they shared their last meal, participated in the spirit of the celebration of the Passover which the first Christian communities were soon to see, as finding its fulfilment in Jesus' Passover: 'Our paschal lamb, Christ, has been sacrificed. Therefore, let us celebrate the festival, not with the old yeast, the yeast of malice and evil, but with the unleavened bread of sincerity and truth' (I Cor 5:7-8).

It was Jesus who, through his Passover, made us free through the New Covenant in his blood.

The Last Supper as Meal

We cannot understand the Last Supper, and the 'founding experience' that it is, for the sacraments of the Eucharist and of Holy Orders, without seeing it as the crowning of all the meals of Jesus' ministry: the Last Supper sums them all up and brings them to fulfilment.

This is an aspect of the Last Supper on which all New Testament sources agree: the Last Supper *was* a meal: the vocabulary of the story in the gospels, in Paul, is abundantly clear: the disciples enquired from Jesus where to make the preparations to eat the Passover (Mk 14:12); they were shown a dining-room where to eat the Passover (Mk 14:14); later on, that day, 'while they were at table eating, Jesus denounced the traitor who was eating with him (Mk 14:18). And it was as they were eating, that he took some bread which he broke and gave to them: 'Take it, he said, this is my body' (Mk 14:22). Then he took a cup, and all drank from it, and he said, 'this is my blood' (Mk 14:24).

John is no less clear than Mark on this: the vocabulary he uses in his discourse on the Bread of Life is even more concrete, we could even say, cruder: 'I tell you most solemnly, if you do not eat (the verb means 'to gnaw, to munch') the flesh of the Son of Man and drink his blood, you will not have life in you' (Jn 6:53). Perhaps a way for John to emphasize the realism of the eucharistic flesh and blood (R. E. Brown, *The Gospel According to John*, Geoffrey Chapman, London 1978, p 283).

As to John's story of the Last Supper, its context is a meal which Jesus shared with his disciples. A meal, that is, a human experience, involving human relationships, human emotions, people relating to one another. And because it was a meal which Jesus shared with his disciples, it had the special quality and flavour attached to Jesus' table-companionship.

The Last Supper was not just a meal where each person present took his, or her own meal, after the manner of a 'self-service' restaurant. Like so many meals in Jesus' ministry, it was a common, a shared meal: Jesus and his disciples sitting at the same table (lying around the same table), eating and drinking, but also speaking to one another; the dialogue going back and forth between Jesus and his disciples; questions put by the disciples to Jesus; arguments between the disciples, and Jesus listening and then giving his own point of view.

The experience of a common meal; an experience which took time; in which feelings were expressed; emotions felt and aired. An experience of communion and sharing; of fellowship expressed and strengthened. From that point of view, John's story is immensely rich, focused as it is on fellowship, on at-oneness.

The Last Supper, a Meal with Sinners

The Last Supper was also a meal with sinners: 'This man welcomes sinners and eats with them' (Lk 15:2).

These words which say so much about Jesus' attitude to sinners during his ministry, are also true of Jesus at the last meal which he shared with his disciples; perhaps, we should say, they are truer than at any other time. And all four gospels make it clear, even Matthew and Luke who tend to hide the weaknesses of the Twelve.

There is, first of all, the presence of Judas, 'about to betray Jesus' (Mk 14:18): there was bound to be a sense of deep shame and distress among the disciples and the early Christians at the thought that one of the Twelve had betrayed his master. The Evangelists, each one in his own way, express those feelings. Matthew and Mark, for instance, place the foretelling of Judas' betrayal by Jesus, just before the 'institution of the Eucharist, and give it a relatively important coverage (Matthew gives it 6 verses out of a total of 10 for the whole story of the Last Supper, Mt 26:20-25; and Mk, 5 verses out of a total of 9, Mk 14:17-21). In both Matthew and Mark, the words of Jesus express his shock and distress at the extreme gravity of what Judas is about to do: there he is, sharing a meal with Jesus and his fellow disciples; sharing once again with them an experience of welcome, of communion, of fellowship, of forgiveness, while having already made up his mind to betray Jesus: 'When it was evening...'

The contrast is shattering between Jesus' words about Judas, 'It would have been better for that man not to have been born', and the story of the institution of the Eucharist which immediately follows: 'While they were eating, he took a loaf of bread, and after blessing it he broke it, gave it to them and said, "Take; this is my body." Then he took a cup, and after giving thanks he gave it to them , and all of them drank from it. He said to them, "This is my blood of the covenant, which is poured out for many. Truly, I tell you, I will never again drink of the fruit of the vine until that day when I drink it new in the kingdom of God' (Mk 14:22-25). Even before Judas was able to carry out his plan to betray him, Jesus gave himself up to him, 'body and blood', as 'food and drink', thus offering Judas a supreme 'covenant-grace.' Jesus, 'the man who welcomes sinners and eats with them.'

Also at table with Jesus was Peter, whose generosity was undeniable, but whose promises often echoed more his self-confidence and pride than his fidelity: 'Even if all lose faith, I will not' (Mk 14:29). At the beginning of Jesus' Passion, Peter will deny his Master.

As to the other disciples who will desert Jesus at the moment of his arrest and run away (Mk 14:50), Luke shows them expressing, as they too share Jesus' last meal, their dreams of power: 'A dispute arose between them about which should be reckoned the greatest' (Lk 22:24).

John sums up, in his own way, the impression that Jesus must have had of his disciples as he was about to leave them: 'The time will come - in fact, it has come already - when you will be scattered each going his own way, and leaving me alone' (Jn 16:32).

We, therefore, understand that the Last Supper was for the disciples, like Jesus' meals during his ministry, an experience of welcome and acceptance. Jesus did not ask them to wear a wedding garment; he simply offered his companionship to them just as they were.

He offered them above all his forgiveness. He knew his disciples well enough to guess what their reaction would be when his enemies put their hands on him - their dreams of power would make his power-lessness before the authorities totally unacceptable. But he loved them, and the Last Meal he could share with them was another opportunity given him to assure them of his love. They had to be sure that, whatever happened, they wouldt remain, as Jesus himself puts it, his friends' (Jn 15:15).

Luke, more than the other Evangelists, comments on this dimension of the Last Supper and he highlights it beautifully in connection with Jesus' dialogue with Peter: 'Simon, Simon, you must know, Satan has got his wish to sift you all like wheat; but I have prayed for you, Simon, that your faith may not fail, and once you have recovered, you in your turn, must strengthen your brothers. Lord, he answered, I would be ready to go to prison with you, and to death. Jesus replied, I tell you, Peter, by the time the cock crows today you will have denied three times that you know me' (Lk 22:31-34).

As I understand this text, that is forgiveness made permanently available, like bread on the table, for whoever will need it. That is what Jesus' meals with sinners were meant to be. And it was in this immense treasure of forgiveness that sinners, including the disciples found the strength to pursue their journey, in spite of their weaknesses and failures.

Yes, truly, one must say of the Jesus of the Last Supper: 'This man welcomes sinners and eats with them.'

Jesus' Words over the Bread and Wine

Jesus' last meal with his disciples was the last in a whole history of meals; it summed them all up as an experience of communion and of forgiveness.

But the New Testament texts invite us to go much further: the Last Supper went far beyond the meals of Jesus' ministry; it revealed their deepest meaning, and their cost for Jesus; it brought Jesus' meals with sinners to fulfilment.

That is perfectly brought out by the words spoken by Jesus as he presented the bread and the cup to his disciples: Then he took some bread, and when he had given thanks, broke it and gave it to them saying, "This is my body which will be given for you, do this as a memorial of me." He did the same with the cup after supper, and said, "This cup is the new covenant in my blood which will be poured out for you"' (Lk 22:19-20).

We have four versions of Jesus' words over the bread and the cup: one in each of the three synoptic gospels – Mt 26:26-29, Mk 14:22-25, Lk 22:19-20 – and one in Paul's first letter to the Corinthians (11:24-25). But – and this is important – these four versions agree completely on the contents of Jesus' words: 'my body for you, my blood for you.'

John, as we know, has not included, in his own story of the Last Supper these words of Jesus. He obviously knew of the Eucharistic tradition in the Christian communities of the first century; and he more than echoes this tradition in his story of the loaves and the discourse on the bread of life which follows this story (Jn 6).

Basically, the Johannine approach expressed in John 6 corresponds to the Synoptic and to the Pauline approach: Jesus' flesh and blood as source of life for those who share in the meal Jesus offers them.

But there is something more in John, and it is of great importance: if John does not have, in his account of the Last Supper, what we call 'the institution of the Eucharist', he opens his account with a story which we do not find in the other gospels: the story of the Washing of the Feet (Jn 13:1-20). The point of that story is clearly indicated in the conclusion found in 13:15: 'I have given you an example so that you may copy what I have done to you'. We could say that these words are John's version of Jesus' 'do this in memory of me.'

The washing of the feet is, for the disciples, an example of humble service. Luke, in his own story of the Last Supper, offers us the same teaching: to the disciples who discuss among themselves 'who should be reckoned the greatest', Jesus says: 'The greatest among you must behave as if he were the youngest, the leader as if he were the one who serves. For who is the greater: the one at table or the one who serves? The one at table, surely,? Yet here am I among you as one who serves' (Lk 2:24-27).

I think that both Luke and John thus draw our attention to the fundamental meaning of Jesus' words over the bread and the cup: Jesus, offering himself as 'bread broken and shared' for the life of the world.

These meals might appear to some as 'a good time spent by Jesus with people of doubtful reputation'; we might be tempted to see them as the easy part in Jesus' ministry. But actually, they expressed Jesus' profound desire, the aim of his mission, to give himself, without reserve, to break down the boundaries which separated people from one another, so that sinners might have life and have it to the full. There is continuity between Jesus sharing meals with sinners, and Jesus saying, 'This is my body for you, take and eat' - the continuity between Jesus' meals with sinners, Jesus' sharing a last meal with his disciples, and Jesus in his Passion; as John puts it: 'He had always loved those who were his in the world, but now he showed how perfect his love was' (Jn 13:1).

How then should we understand the words over the bread and the cup? They are words over bread and wine to be shared; words which point out to a meal, to the human, basic, experience of a meal. And therefore, it will be through the experience of a meal, the human experience of a meal, that the disciples will have access to the mystical reality expressed by the words. Reducing the human experience of a meal to its barest minimum will not enhance the mystical reality it is meant to carry. It will, on the contrary, make it more difficult to perceive; it will make it into a skeleton without flesh. Symbols are not meant to be an empty reality; on the contrary, they are meant to point to it, to express it in a rich, attractive, human way.

I feel that just as we do not give more chance to Jesus' divinity if we diminish or empty his humanness, in the same way, we do not give more chance to the body and blood of the Lord, if we decide to reduce the breadness of the bread, or the wineness of the wine; or if we reduce to an austere and bare ritual the meal in which the bread and wine are meant to be shared.

As words over food to be shared and eaten, over wine to be shared and drunk, Jesus' words send us back to his meals, and therefore are an invitation to communion, to welcoming sinners, to respecting them; an invitation to a celebration of forgiveness. Hearing these words against the background music of Jesus' meals does not impoverish them, does not 'secularize' them: it makes them bearers of the richness of Jesus' ministry of reconciliation and life.

Jesus' words are also (and here lies their tremendous newness) about Jesus giving himself, 'body and blood', 'flesh and blood'; Jesus accepting, in the Upper Room, to go to the very end of his love for his disciples, for the world; going to the end of the journey begun in Bethlehem and Nazareth, through Galilee, and Judaea. Jesus at the Last Supper, already entering his Passion, his Passover. Through these words, Jesus' ministry and especially Jesus' meals are integrated, so to speak, in his Passion; they are revealed as, Jesus' Passion, Jesus' supreme sacrifice, in the making. Through Jesus' words over the bread and the cup, it is the whole life of Jesus, his whole ministry, and especially his meals with sinners, which become promoted to the dignity and richness of his Passover.

'Do this in memory of me'

Presenting the first Christian communities in Jerusalem, Luke writes in the Acts of the Apostles: 'These remained faithful to the teaching of the Apostles, to the brotherhood, to the breaking of bread and to the prayers' (Acts 2:42).

Thus, in the first Christian communities, the faithful did continue to participate in the Temple liturgy, but they also met together in their houses to celebrate the Risen Lord, and that celebration included in particular 'the breaking of bread', that is, a meal shared 'in memory of Jesus.' At the source of this specifically Christian ritual, there was, obviously, the last meal shared by Jesus with his disciples before his Passion: but a meal which, as we have seen, summed up and crowned Jesus' table-companionship during his ministry.

How should we understand Jesus' words today when we celebrate the Eucharist?

'Do this in memory of me': to whom are these words addressed?

The Christian theological tradition has seen in Jesus' words, 'Do this in memory of me', words addressed, in the first place to the apostles as the founders of the first Christian communities; words which 'found' the Christian priesthood, and therefore the power to repeat what Jesus had done and said at the Last Supper.

We must add, however, that these words extend Jesus' invitation, beyond the apostles and their successors, to all his disciples who, through their baptism, have a share in Jesus' priesthood. But in what sense do the words concern them?

An Invitation to Remember

'Do this in memory of me': the Eucharist is the great moment when, guided by Spirit who is 'God's memory in us' (Jn 14:26) we are invited to remember Jesus, to focus again our minds and hearts and lives in Jesus 'who leads us in our faith and brings it to perfection' (Heb 12:2), whose mystery becomes reality here and now.

But what is the 'this' that we must do 'in memory of Jesus'? The words 'do this in memory of me' refer of course first to what Jesus said and did at the Last Supper. They are an invitation given to the Church to re-live faithfully the founding experience which the institution of the Eucharist was.

But Jesus' words go obviously beyond the simple ritual of the Eucharist. This is expressed beautifully during the ceremony of

Priestly Ordination, in the words spoken by the ordaining bishop to the deacons he is empowering to celebrate the Eucharist: 'Imitate, live out, what you are doing' (imitamini quod tractatis, as the Latin ritual had it). 'Do this,' that is, let what you are doing in the celebration of the Eucharist be your mission, your life; be willing to be 'bread broken and shared' that the world may live, in memory of me.

We must go further: it was of course through his passover, passion, death and resurrection, that Jesus became 'bread broken and shared' for the world, 'for the forgiveness of sins.' But Jesus' passion was the culmination of a life lived 'for others'; so that the 'this' of Jesus' invitation, 'Do this in memory of me' extends to his whole life, to his whole ministry.

We are thus drawn into the movement, the dynamics of Jesus' Passover; drawn into joining 'sinners', the sinners we all are, in answering Jesus' invitation, in accepting, welcoming his kindness and mercy, his forgiveness; in sharing them with one another, as we share the bread and wine, in communion with him and with one another; as we share the body and blood that the bread and wine have become. There must be no limit to our sharing, just as there was no limit to Jesus' sharing. The Eucharist is therefore a most challenging experience, a most radical stand taken in our communities, a programme embracing our whole life.

It is a programme in which communion-making, boundary-breaking will always be a priority, because they are at all times a most urgent need in the world; and because they were already the priority of Jesus' life, beginning with 'the bite and scandal' of Jesus' table-companionship: 'A glutton and a drunkard, a friend of tax collectors and sinners' (Mt 11:19); '… this man welcomes sinners and eats with them' (Lk 15:2).

It is a most demanding programme also because it touches the whole network of our relationships within our families and communities, within society at large, and of course between the Christian Churches whom 'the problem' of table-companionship continues to keep apart from each other. We cannot be content with feeling the pain of separation, and divisions: every time we celebrate the Eucharist, we are invited to commit ourselves anew to being with Jesus, bridge-

builders, whatever the cost. Guided by the Spirit, strengthened by the
Body and Blood of the Lord, we will find in our own hearts, the
words, gestures, and attitudes which will make all the members of our
Christian communities feel welcomed, whether they wear the wedding garment or not. It is the Father's will that the banquet room be
full.

CHAPTER FIVE

The Risen Lord, Recognized in the Breaking of Bread
The Emmaus Story

We find, in the Acts of the Apostles, a rather surprising statement made by Peter in the course of a 'catechesis' which he gave, in Caesarea, to a Roman officer and to his family. Speaking about Jesus, Peter said, 'God raised him on the third day and allowed him to appear, not to all the people but to us who were chosen by God as witnesses, and who ate and drank with him after he rose from the dead. He commanded us to preach to the people and to testify that he is the one ordained by God as judge of the living and the dead.' (Acts 10:40-42)

What was the place of meals in the experience which the disciples were given of the presence of the Risen Lord? What light does it shed on our Eucharist?

A First Contact with the Texts

A quick survey shows that there are mainly four texts in the New Testament in which the disciples' experience of their encounter with the Risen Lord is connected in some way with a meal.

i) Luke 24:28-32 – the experience of the two disciples met by the Risen Lord on the way to Emmaus. This encounter culminated in a meal.
ii) Luke 24:41-42 – an encounter between the Risen Lord and the

disciples in Jerusalem; an encounter which includes a meal. iii) John 21:10-12 - an encounter between the Risen Lord and seven disciples on the shore of Lake Tiberias. John shows Jesus inviting his disciples for a meal. iv) Acts 10:40-42 – Peter's testimony quoted above.

We can set apart immediately the text of Acts 10:41; the core of the story to which it belongs is a catechesis in which Peter presents to his host, a Roman officer, the Good News of Jesus. It resembles the catecheses found in the 'speeches of the Acts' (2:14-36; 4:5-12; 13:16-37).

These speeches probably represent an early stage in the development of Christian catechesis; they tend to be factual; and that is certainly the case of Peter's catechesis in Acts 10 – John's baptism, Jesus' ministry in Galilee, and then in Judaea and Jerusalem; Jesus' death on the cross; and, to conclude, the experience of witnesses who 'saw' Jesus alive: meals with, or in the presence of, the Risen Lord were part of that experience. It is interesting to note that in Peter's catechesis in Acts 10, all these facts are put, or at least presented, as if they were on the same level of 'historicity. And that might be important.

But what about the other texts, especially the Emmaus story in Luke 24:13-35? These texts, too, are stories which are basically catecheses. In these stories, the evangelist's intention is not only to affirm that Jesus is alive, but also to show what Jesus' resurrection means for the disciples in terms of daily living: these catecheses are about the journey of the Easter faith. Their insistence is less on the person of the Risen Lord than on the disciples' response to his presence.

To say that these stories are catecheses does not mean that they are not related to historical experiences. The encounters between the Risen Lord and his disciples, whatever their nature, necessarily took place in circumstances of time and place. Circumstances which may very well form the backbone of the Resurrection narratives; thus Luke would use the experience of two disciples met by the Risen Lord as they were on their way to Emmaus in order to present a detailed catechesis on the Easter faith.

If this approach is correct, we can say that it may be historically significant that the Resurrection narratives point out several times to a meal as the human context of the encounter between the Risen Lord and his disciples. Meals, as we know, were privileged moments in Jesus' ministry; experiences of welcome, of acceptance, of communion, of forgiveness. As such, meals characterised Jesus' mission, his style: 'This man welcomes sinners and eats with them' (Lk 15:2). Was it not normal, therefore, – even necessary – that the encounters between the Risen Lord and his disciples should have been connected with meals?

The Emmaus Story (Luke 24:13-35)

With all this in mind, let us then assume, for simplicity's sake, that on Easter morning, two disciples left Jerusalem to go to Emmaus; on their way, they were met by the Risen Lord; when they went back to Jerusalem, they shared their experience with the other disciples. Luke, later, used their story in order to present a fairly extensive catechesis on the meaning of Jesus' resurrection. In other words, the present Emmaus story in Luke's gospel, aims at answering important and necessary questions which we are bound to ask ourselves: If we are serious about being Christians, where can we find the Risen Lord in our life, what are the signs of his presence, and what does his resurrection mean for us in terms of daily living?

One of the most striking features in the Emmaus story is the importance of the vocabulary of 'journeying': two men on their way to a village called Emmaus are joined by a third man; towards evening they stop in an inn for a meal, and then resume their journey – a journey which is not simply geographical but also a spiritual venture. We could say that Luke outlines before us, in the Emmaus story, the journey of the Easter faith, the journey of discipleship.

Luke seems to highlight especially four major experiences in the disciples' journey.

First Experience: a Companion on the Road (Luke 24:13-24)

'Two disciples were on their way to a village called Emmaus.' Their minds and hearts were full of the very distressful experience of the last few days: the crucifixion and death of Jesus of Nazareth, their master; Jesus who, they had hoped, would be the Messiah who would make Israel free. He had called them, they had answered his call, they had followed him, of glorious dreams about the future, their future. But now, it was all over: Jesus' death had sealed his total failure. And they had deserted him at the moment he was arrested, and they had run away, leaving him alone to face his enemies, to face death.

The distress of dreams that have been destroyed! The distress of guilt, of shame for having let down, miserably, a Master, a friend. The two disciples were plunged in their own 'passion'; leaving Jerusalem was for them a way of escaping a situation which had turned into a disaster.

And it was from this 'now', laden with sadness, disappointment, and guilt, that the Easter journey began for them. The Risen Lord met them where they were, at the heart of their 'passion', of their distress. That is the meaning of his resurrection: to be with us , wherever we may be; to wait for us wherever distress and pain, and guilt, assail us. And to be with us as a companion.

As a 'companion', not as a judge; nor as a spectator either. The companion of the two disciples on the road to Emmaus did not immediately start teaching them, giving them a lesson. On the contrary, he invited them to express their feelings; he could thus enter into their own minds and hearts, so to speak, and suffer with them their 'passion.' What seemed immediately important to him was not that they should recognise him as the Risen Lord, but rather that they could share with him, on the road, their distress. He let them be themselves; he invited them to be themselves; he accepted them, welcomed them as they were. A true companion indeed.

Second Experience: the Experience of the Scriptures

On the road on which the disciples had followed Jesus of Nazareth, they had met a major obstacle; an obstacle which finally had caused them to lose their way: the cross! Jesus' cross, and the failure it symbolised; the death it led to; death with its finality: 'Two whole days have gone by since it all happened... Of him, they saw nothing' (Lk 24:21, 24).

But whatever the crosses we have to carry as we journey on, the Risen Lord is with us as our companion. And gently, lovingly, he tries to help us on our way, to help us find meaning through it all; he offers us the light of the Scriptures: 'You are so slow to believe the full meaning of the prophets. Was it not ordained that the Christ should suffer, and so enter into his glory? Then starting with Moses, and going through all the prophets, he explained to them the passages throughout the scriptures, that were about himself' (Lk 24:25-27).

But how can the Scriptures help us in our journey? The scriptures are all about the life-journey of God's People: they tell us again and again that whatever the experiences of sin, of pain and failure, and distress and death which marked Israel's faith-journey, nothing was ever wasted. God, in his love, cancelled nothing, but redeemed all into life. It was also Jesus' experience; and his resurrection was, for Jesus himself, the supreme sign of God's victory over all forces of evil and death.

And so, the scriptures which had mapped out Jesus' own journey, map out ours too. Read in the light of Easter, they will not change the reality of our lives, of our journey. But they can renew our vision of reality; they can help us understand, as they helped the two disciples on the road to Emmaus, that the cross is not just an obstacle; but that it is also, that it can be, a life-giving experience; an experience which offers new possibilities for loving, for growing. In Paul's words, the cross is 'the power of God and the wisdom of God' (I Cor 1:24).

Third Experience: Bread Broken and Shared (Luke 24:28-35)

In the unfolding of the journey of the disciples whom the Risen Lord met on the road, 'the breaking of bread' appears like the 'key-experience' which, in some way, sums up for the two of them, 'what had happened on the road' (Lk 24:35). Both the stranger who had joined them as they walked away from Jerusalem, and the 'exegete' who 'had talked to them on the road and explained the scriptures to them' (v 32) had been a marvellous companion: 'he had set their hearts burning'; and as they invited him to stay on with them, they expressed their desire to know more about him; they wanted him to prolong the companionship he had offered them. Yet, in some way, he was still a stranger to them. The moment of revelation was the meal he shared with them.

Let us read attentively Luke's story of that meal: 'As they came near the village to which they were going, he walked ahead as if he were going on. But they urged him strongly, saying, "Stay with us, because it is almost evening and the day is now nearly over." So he went in to stay with them. When he was at the table with them, he took bread, blessed and broke it, and gave it to them. Then their eyes were opened, and they recognized him; and he vanished from their sight. They said to each other, "Were not our hearts burning within us while he was talking to us on the road, while he was opening the scriptures to us?" That same hour they got up and returned to Jerusalem... Then they told what had happened on the road, and how he had been made known to them in the breaking of the bread (Lk 24:28-35)

Jesus' meal with the two disciples is given, in Luke's story, a relatively lengthy treatment; for the two disciples it was truly the very heart of their experience: 'They had recognised him at the breaking of bread' (Lk 19:35). Why was this simple meal so 'revealing' an experience for them?

A Typical Meal of Jesus, the 'revealing' sign of the Risen Lord

About Jesus during his ministry, people said, 'This man welcomes sinners and eats with them' (Lk 15:2). It is just as true of the Risen Lord: in this sense that the Risen Lord is Jesus of Nazareth today; the 'today' of the two disciples on the road; our own 'today.' Jesus, who is the great 'healer', Jesus who accepts, welcomes people without any preconditions, who takes them where they are, offers them the healing of his presence, the healing of forgiveness, of communion, not as pre-conditions, but as the on-going experience in which the disciples are be made stronger to continue their journey. And in that experience, the meal is a key-moment; a moment of special intimacy; a moment which lasts, in which love has time to grow, to feel at home; a moment where healing and communion are given a chance to grow deeper.

'They recognised him...' That is an extraordinary statement. Actually the whole sentence is extraordinary: 'Their eyes were opened, and they recognised him, but he had vanished from their sight' (Lk 24:31).

It was then, and then only, 'in the breaking of bread', that the two disciples recognised Jesus: this is brought out twice, in vv 31 and 35. Luke really wants us to pay attention to this.

Why is Luke led to say that? Should we speak simply of Jesus' special way of 'breaking the bread' when he shared a meal with people, with his disciples? Surely, Luke wants us to go deeper: it was not just the way, the gesture; it was what they stood for, what they symbolised: Jesus' love for meals shared with people, with sinners, with people on the margins. The two disciples Jesus had met on the road were burdened with sorrow, they had been cowards, they had left him alone, they had not believed in him. And now, they came to realize that Jesus was alive, that he was with them. Through the breaking of bread, they were shown, by the stranger met on the road, that 'his body had truly been broken for them, for the forgiveness of their sins.' And so, the 'breaking of bread' in the inn identified in the eyes of the two disciples, the Jesus of the ministry who 'welcomed sinners and ate with them', the Jesus of the Last Supper who had given himself for the forgiveness of sins; the Jesus of the Passion who had been broken that they might live.

'But he had vanished from their sight...' (Lk 24:31). What does Luke mean? It is the only expression of this sort that we find in the Resurrection narratives: the sudden 'being there' of the Risen Lord is alluded to several times (see Lk 24:36; Jn 20:14; 20:19; 21:4). But nothing is said of the disappearing: it seems to be taken for granted.

What then does Luke want to say? Theologically, we must obviously say that the Risen Lord, because he is now alive with God's life, is always there. Once again, that is what the resurrection is about in terms of daily living. Therefore, his 'appearances' are 'outward manifestations' of his permanent presence; they are like the tip of the iceberg: they signify, they highlight the permanent reality of the Risen Lord's presence.

That was the effect of the breaking of bread for the disciples: it identified the reality and presence of the Risen Lord, it made it real, highlighting what was already there.

And since they now knew, in faith, that Jesus was risen, there was no point, so to speak, for him 'to stay around in a visible manner'; he was with them, they knew it. He, therefore, 'vanished from their sight', while remaining their ever-present companion.

Fourth Experience: 'They set out that instant...'

All the encounters between the Risen Lord and his disciples lead the latter to mission; as Peter and John put it before the Sanhedrin, 'we cannot promise to stop proclaiming what we have seen and heard' (Acts 4:20), the 'inner compulsion' of the experience of the presence of the Risen Lord.

In Luke, the disciples' mission is brought out explicitly in 24:47-49. But it is at least suggested in the Emmaus story. The encounter with the Risen Lord has so renewed the disciples' heart that they cannot wait to go back to Jerusalem and to the disciples' community there.

For what purpose? 'They told their story of what had happened on the road, and how they had recognised him in the breaking of bread' (Lk 24:35).

A mission which meant, therefore, sharing; sharing the experience given them by the Risen Lord; the very experience which the disciples in Jerusalem share with them on their arrival there: 'They found the eleven assembled together with their companions who said to them: yes, it is true, the Lord has risen and has appeared to Simon' (Lk 24:33-34). That is, at the heart of the disciples' mission, we find the Risen Lord, and the sacrament of his presence, the breaking of bread.

CONCLUSION

The encounter with the Risen Lord was, for the two disciples, a journey; it was a unique, exceptional moment in a journey which had begun long before they had even met Jesus of Nazareth; a journey destined to continue until the Risen Lord welcomed them into his Father's house (Jn 14:3).

During Jesus' ministry, they had often shared meals with Jesus, and from him they had always received respect, welcome, forgiveness, communion. And they, in their turn, had shared respect, welcome, forgiveness, communion with so many people, especially marginalised, sinners.

Until the evening when, in Jerusalem, they had shared a last meal: the meal during which he had told them of his love for them, love to the end: 'my body for you, my blood for you.' They had not really understood these mysterious words then. And when, after supper, they had left the Upper Room to go to Gethsemane, they had sensed something terrible was about to happen, but without really grasping what it would be. And then there had been Jesus' arrest, and they had all run away. And for the next three days, it had been through the reports of the women that they had learnt about Jesus' condemnation, and his crucifixion. The horror of those days! Until, on the third day, brushing away the rumours reported by the women that Jesus was alive, they had decided to take to the road again, but this time, without Jesus; they had to go away, and sort things out, and involve themselves in something else.

And the encounter on the road! And the kind stranger joining them, and listening to their litany of woes, and trying to bolster up their hopes through the scriptures. And the great moment had come: the meal and the breaking of bread. And now, they knew he was alive, they knew he had forgiven them, that he had truly given them the greatest proof that a friend can give to those he loves, the gift of his life.

'Do this in memory of me': to celebrate the Eucharist is, for us today, to enter into the experience of the two disciples on their way to Emmaus; a moment of revelation when we celebrate the presence of the Risen Lord, our companion on our journey; a moment when, together, we listen to the Word of God in the scriptures, and thus learn anew to read our own lives in their light; a moment when Jesus the Risen Lord 'takes the bread, says the blessing, breaks the bread saying, take and eat, this is my Body for you, for the forgiveness of sin; go and do this in memory of me.'

CHAPTER SIX

The Lord's Supper in the First Christian Communities

'Do this in memory of me': these are the words which were meant to be the bond between the various steps of our reflections on Jesus' table-companionship. We wanted to find out what 'this' could mean. And our investigation took us back to Jesus' ministry in Galilee and to the meals he shared with people; it took us to the Upper Room where Jesus shared a last meal with his disciples; it took us finally to the road on which two disciples were walking, away from Jerusalem, on Easter Day.

It is precisely on the Eucharist itself that we are now going to focus our minds. So that when 'we do this in memory of Jesus', we may do it more conscious of the tremendous experience we celebrate, more aware also of the challenges it offers us.

If we wanted to express in a few words what Jesus, the table-companion, wanted to reveal about God, we could simply quote the conclusion of 'the parable of the Banquet' in Luke's gospel: 'Go to the open roads and the hedgerows and press people to come in, to make sure my house is full; because I tell you, not one of those who were invited shall have a taste of my banquet' (Lk 14:23-24).

If it is left to Jesus, and to the God whom he came to reveal, then, the hall will be filled to capacity, not by spectators, but by people 'coming from east and west and sitting down with Abraham, Isaac and Jacob at the feast of the Kingdom of Heaven' (Mt 8:11).

Of course, people can always refuse to accept the permanent invitation offered them by God; they can use their freedom to excommunicate themselves. But they will never be able to invoke their poverty, their misery, their sinfulness to stay away; for Jesus, in God's name, always 'welcomes sinners and eats with them' (Lk 15:2).

Does that mean that there are no limits to taking part in the banquet of the Kingdom? Matthew's gospel, through the parable of the Wedding Garment (Mt 22:14), seems to say that such limits do exist. But what is the 'wedding garment' of the parable, concretely? Perhaps can we find light on this in Paul's first letter to the Christians of Corinth.

The Celebration of the Lord's Supper at Corinth

In the Acts of the Apostles, Luke refers several times to the practice of the 'Breaking of Bread' in the Christian community in Jerusalem: 'They devoted themselves to the apostles' teaching and fellowship, to the breaking of bread and the prayers... Day by day, as they spent much time together in the temple, they broke bread at home and ate their food with glad and generous hearts (Acts 2:42-46).

We do not know for certain whether the 'breaking of bread' in this text refers to the celebration of the Lord's Supper, or simply to a fraternal meal shared by the members of the Jerusalem Christian community 'in memory of Jesus' table-companionship.' What seems to be certain is that the expression came to imply 'the eucharistic ceremony' (see I Cor 10:16; 11:24, and the footnotes in the Jerusalem Bible).

Or, as Paul calls it in I Cor 11, 'the Lord's Supper.' Paul, here, is a most important witness: he wrote his first letter to the Christians of Corinth around the year 57 A.D., that is, about twenty or thirty years before Luke wrote his gospel and the Acts of the Apostles. In other words, through Paul, we come into contact with the very first Christian communities, about twenty five years after Pentecost. In I Cor, Paul speaks at some length about the celebration of the Lord's Supper in Corinth (I Cor 11:17-32).

It was not a celebration which Paul himself had introduced in the Christian communities he had founded, independently from the tradition of other Christian communities. On the contrary, Paul insists that his stand is that of Christian tradition: 'For this is what I received from the Lord and in turn passed on to you' (I Cor 11:23).

How did the Corinthians celebrate the Lord's Supper? As far as we can make out from Paul's text, the custom seems to have been to celebrate the Lord's Supper in private homes; and the celebration included a fraternal meal which led up to the ritual of the Lord's Supper – a beautiful custom which kept alive the memory of Jesus who sat at table with people to offer them an experience of communion and forgiveness.

So as not to overburden the host-family, it was agreed that each one would bring some food which would be shared by all the guests. A truly fraternal meal, a shared meal, which was a splendid, concrete preparation for the celebration of the Lord's Supper.

But abuses had crept into the Corinthian community: the way the Lord's Supper was celebrated was marked by an unacceptable paradox: on the one hand, the Corinthians were supposed to share a meal, and therefore enter fully into the spirit of a shared meal, the way Jesus did when he shared meals with people. The celebration of the Lord's Supper in Corinth was meant to be a family, a community celebration: 'When you come together as a community' (I Cor 11:18).

On the other hand, however, it was obvious that community meetings in Corinth did more harm than good: there were separate factions, one person went hungry while another was getting drunk; the result being that people were embarrassed. In other words, in Corinth, the celebration of the Lord's Supper was exactly the opposite of what it was meant to be; as Paul puts it, 'It is not the Lord's Supper' (I Cor 11:20).

The abuse in Corinth was not a matter of ritual; it was the spirit in which the celebration was conducted that was unacceptable. Paul tried to change it. He first invited Christians to go back to the founding experience which the Last Supper was, to go back to Jesus: 'On the night he was betrayed...' (I Cor 11:23-25).

Thus in the course of the last meal which he shared with his disciples before his Passion, Jesus already offered himself body and soul *for* them; and to celebrate the Lord's Supper was to 'do this in memory of him' (11:24-25). Consequently, one should ponder and reflect before entering into the movement of Jesus' Passover: 'Everyone is to recollect himself before eating this bread and drinking this cup; because a person who eats and drinks without recognising the body is eating and drinking his own condemnation' (I Cor 28-29).

Paul's words must be understood properly: Paul has in mind someone who is taking part in the Lord's Supper, and who therefore 'eats this bread and drinks this cup'. That person, Paul says, must ponder, recollect himself/herself, before eating the Body and drinking the Blood of Christ. That is, that person must first recognise 'the body': we must note that Paul does not write that one should 'recognise the Body and the Blood'; he uses the word 'body' all by itself; which means that Paul does not have in mind only the Eucharistic Body of Christ. What he has in mind, first and foremost, is 'the body that the Christian community is' (I Cor 12:27).

In other words, the celebration of the Lord's Supper demands, on the part of Christians, that they be inspired by Jesus' spirit: the spirit of Jesus 'who welcomed sinners and ate with them'; the spirit of Jesus sharing a last meal with his disciples, before he entered into his Passion; the spirit of the Risen Lord who met his disciples after the Resurrection. The spirit of welcome, communion, forgiveness, of love and mercy. To be community conscious, to refuse any form of discrimination are not just possibilities for anyone participating in the Lord's Supper; they are essential.

And therefore, there are people whom Paul would exclude - or more accurately, who would exclude themselves - from the Lord's Supper; people who, in some way or other, refuse to join the community, people who do not want the community. Those are people who do not have the wedding garment, and do not want any.

The Eucharist in our Communities Today

In the light of all this, we understand that in order to know exactly what 'doing this in memory of me' means in terms of daily living, we must go back to the very source of the Church's eucharistic tradition, to Jesus himself.

Jesus' mission, his supreme priority, was to reveal God as a God of mercy and compassion, as 'Abba.' As Jesus himself expresses it, 'the whole world must be brought to know that I love the Father and that I do exactly what he commands me' (Jn 14:31). And the Father's will was, and is, that all his children may have life and have it to the full (Jn 10:10); that they all may be one (17:11). Not just life eternal, up there, but life here and now, for all the Father's children; life growing towards fulness. To participate in the Eucharist is to let Jesus' mission and priority sink ever deeper roots into our own hearts.

Jesus fulfilled his mission through his teaching, through his healing ministry, and especially through the meals he shared with people. Meals were for Jesus moments, experiences of welcome, forgiveness, of communion. They were Abba's loving kindness made real for people who sat at table with Jesus.

Not just for some people, for people who observed the Law, for people who belonged to the in-group of Jewish religious society. On the contrary, Jesus' meals, while open to all, were offered by priority to sinners, the marginalized; people whose lives and hearts were touched by the sickness of sin, of ignorance; people who needed healing: 'This man welcomes sinners and eats with them' (Lk 15:2). There was no room for discrimination in Jesus' table-companionship; there should not be any either in our celebration of the Eucharist.

But are there 'sinners, marginalized people' in our Christian communities today? People we discriminate against in our families, in our communities, in society at large? People we discriminate against in the celebration of the Eucharist? We must not too easily say that we have good, holy reasons to discriminate against certain people. There has been much ambiguity on this point in the Church's history; an ambiguity which Jesus' disciples experienced even while he was still with them: 'We saw a man casting out devils in your name, and because he is not with us, we tried to stop him. But Jesus said to him (John), "You must not stop him; anyone who is not against you is for you"' (Lk 9:49-50)

I am personally convinced that in some way, discrimination is deeply ingrained in us, in our communities, our families, today, just as much as yesterday. So deeply ingrained that we easily come to think that it is the expression of God's will, that God is on our side. And yet, is it not true that, at times, we practise discrimination also for selfish reasons, because we feel threatened by 'otherness', by 'difference', and we want to protect ourselves, to erect boundaries around us which will make us feel good.

The celebration of the Eucharist 'in memory of Jesus' challenges us; it asks us to make of our lives a memorial of him, to be Jesus in the world today, the Jesus who 'welcomes sinners and eats with them.' As we celebrate the Eucharist, we are called to renew our commitment to be truly Jesus' disciples; to take part fully in Jesus' mission, and therefore, to be, like him, 'boundary-breakers', 'communion-makers', seeking, like Jesus, to offer welcome, forgiveness, healing to all. Whatever the cost: 'My Body for you, my Blood for you'.

Writing about the tremendous achievement of Jesus' mission in bringing together Jews and pagans, the author of the Letter to the Ephesians draws our attention to the price Jesus accepted to pay to bring about communion and unity: 'Now, in Christ Jesus, you that use to be so far apart from us (the Jews) have been brought very close by the blood of Christ… He is the peace between us. He has made us into one… by destroying in his own person the hostility' (Eph 2:13-14).

'In his own person, he destroyed the hostility': the Eucharist is the sacrament of Jesus' mission of unity; and therefore, the celebration of the Eucharist, the various forms of 'Eucharistic devotions', must be understood as our response to the Risen Lord's constant invitation to commit ourselves anew do 'doing this in memory of him'.

The journey of discipleship is a difficult and long journey, because it means 'following Jesus.' But the Jesus who says, 'Come, follow me, do this in memory of me', is the Risen Lord, our constant companion. The celebration of the Lord's Supper is, in our communities, the celebration of his constant presence at our side; the presence, not of the judge, but of the companion who welcomes us, forgives us, strengthens us, so that we may walk on 'in memory of him.' Until he comes to take us with him into the Father's home.

Saint Dominic
and the Order of Preachers

Simon Tugwell OP

Some saints attract veneration even during their lifetime and leave behind, in the imagination of succeeding ages, a vivid remembrance of who they were. Others are more self-effacing: it is as if they hide behind the works they leave behind them and the ideals which they prompted others to follow. Saint Dominic was one such saint: when he died in 1221, the order which he had established, the Order of Preachers, commonly known as the Dominicans, buried him, sadly and affectionately, and then got on with the job he had given them.

This book tells the story of Dominic and of the work he founded, with full-colour illustrations – from the medieval *Nine Ways of Parayer of Saint Dominic*, and from present-day Dominican artists Mary Grace Thul and Albert Carpentier.

Simon Tugwell OP, a member of the English Province, works in the Historical Institute of the Order in Rome. His books include *The Way of the Preacher* (1979), and *Early Dominicans* which he edited for the Classics of Western Spirituality series.

ISBN 1-871552-78-8   215 x 138 mm

48 pages   Paperback   Full-colour illustrations

€6.34

Dominican Publications
42 Parnell Square
Dublin 1

www.dominicanpublications.com
info@dominicanpublications.com

Strands from a Tapestry
A STORY OF DOMINICAN SISTERS
IN LATIN AMERICA

Mary O Byrne OP

In 1967, three sisters from the then autonomous, semi-enclosed Taylor's Hill convent in Galway set out for Argentina to investigate the possibility of opening a mission there. This book tells the story of what resulted from that journey.

The sisters started their work in Argentina by administering the school in the Keating Institute in Buenos Aires. When Taylor's Hill joined the Cabra Congregation of Dominican Sisters, others joined the Argentine adventure and the work was expanded. The decision to move into direct evangelisation through pastoral work in the *barrios* brought the sisters into even more direct involvement in the lives of the people.

The story of the sisters' life and work is interwoven with the story of the poor of Argentina and with an account of the changes brought about by the renewal movement in religious life. These linked stories put the reader in contact with the challenge of moving beyond traditional frontiers into new places, and of taking up new ways of praying, living and preaching the liberating message of the Gospel.

Mary O Byrne, a member of the Cabra Congregation of Dominican Sisters, has worked in Argentina for twenty-one years. There she learned to know and love the people of Latin America and their culture, and became aware of the stand the Dominicans made in colonial times against the injustices and cruelty of the conquistadors. She also experienced at first hand the patience and tenacity of poor people in present-day Argentina.

ISBN 1-871552-79-6   215 x 138 mm

304 pages   Paperback   Full-colour illustrations Maps   €16.49

Dominican Publications, 42 Parnell Square, Dublin

Dominican Publications

publish the following journals:
Doctrine & Life,

Religious Life Review,

Scripture in Church,

Spirituality.

We also publish, or stock, a limited number of books.
For information about subscribing, and buying, visit our
website:

www.dominicanpublications.com
info@dominicanpublications.com